FIRST
WORLD
PROBLEMS

FIRST WORLD PROBLEMS

Illustrations by
Gemma Correl

weldon**owen**

WHAT'S THE POINT of living in FRANCE if there's no HULU?

THE HEADPHONES SAY "NOISE CANCELING,"

but I can still hear stuff.

GOLDEN DELICIOUS APPLES?

Where's my locally sourced pesticide-free early-harvest heirloom Hubbardston's Nonesuch Pippins?

Not enough gold to buy my elflord a new warhammer.

SPENT WEEKS ON MY SAILOR MOON COSTUME.

IT'S THE **WORST** ONE AT COMIC-CON.

Six years to write a sequel? REALLY?

FaceTime
makes
me look
horrible.

My new HDTV
is too thin.
The Wii sensor
keeps falling off.

I ENTERED MY ZIP CODE WRONG AT THE GAS PUMP.

Oh god, now I have to go inside and talk to a human being.

Siri doesn't understand me. And I'm not even SCOTTISH.

Still haven't gotten over *Firefly* being canceled.

The Walking Dead was on an hour ago. Why isn't it on Netflix yet?

He said he was into animation.

How was I supposed to know that meant COSPLAYING as MY LITTLE PONY?

OH SHIT.

That muffin was technically FOUR SERVINGS.

Paid for the all-you-can-eat buffet. Full after ONE plate. Of SALAD.

20 NUGGETS.

ONE DIPPING SAUCE.

What the hell?

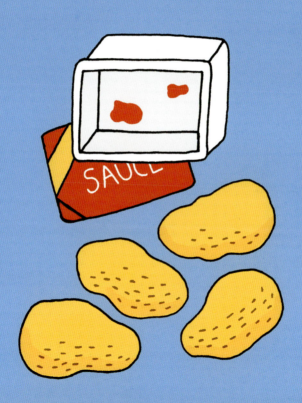

My mom is reading
Fifty Shades of Grey.

I want to
read outside,
but the
glare
washes
out my
screen.

I just **KNOW** the nail salon employees are talking about me . . .

...but I don't even
know what language
they're speaking.

The neighbors just
password-protected
their Wi-Fi.

Pressing
control+click
to right-click
is STUPID.

These ads are
NOT RELEVANT
to my interests.

NO 3G
IN THE
OFFICE
BATHROOM.

OH MY GOD.

This is totally KHAKI.

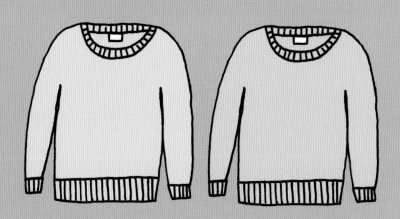

The website
CLEARLY
said "Ecru."

EW,
non-dairy
creamer.

What!? There's totally foam in my no-foam pumpkin-caramel latte.

Separating the recycling is so BORING.

Why can't they do that at the recycling center?

I can't decide between Durango Dusk, Cornsilk, or Montauk Driftwood for the walls of my MUDROOM.

LOST MY PHONE.

If my friend tries calling me to help locate it, he'll hear that my ringtone for him is "Never Let You Go" and I'll never live it down.

Being a
LOCAVORE
means I can't
drink my Fiji
Water.

Perrier in a
plastic bottle
tastes
WEIRD.

Favorite band
is playing on
the main stage.

Boyfriend's crappy
band is on at the same
time on second stage.

My treadmill broke.
Now I have to run
OUTDOORS.

Bluetooth headset died halfway through workout. Condemned to 30 minutes of SILENCE.

Why don't any of the free-range organic unpasturized cage-free eggs have white shells?

Brown shells
are ICKY.

Watched TV stoned. Forgot to fast-forward through commercials.

WASTED MINUTES OF MY LIFE.

My microwave offers me
TOO MANY
OPTIONS.

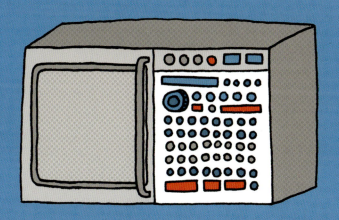

There's like,

TWO

chocolate chips
in this whole
damn cookie.

Gourmet,
my ass.

No Dr. Pepper®.
Only Mr. Pibb®.

Iceberg lettuce
on my $14 sandwich.

This **Swedish** furniture is too confusing to assemble.

My cookie is too big to dunk in my milk.

Stupid pregnant lady getting on the train.

Have to give her my seat or EVERYONE will glare at me.

NPR pledge drive?
But I wanted to
hear Fresh Air!

Bon Jovi?
CLASSIC ROCK?
Really?

Autocorrect keeps changing my swear words.

I'm tired of these motherfunky snakes on this monkeyducking plane.

EAT A BAG OF DOCKS

But never into anything funny enough to post.

The train's Wi-Fi is slower than 3G.

Edge network? really?
What year is this,
1637?

PEOPLE KEEP ADDING ME TO THEIR CIRCLES ON GOOGLE+.

How the hell do I fold fitted sheets?

Wait, irons have settings?

In the middle of a VERY IMPORTANT raid. Girlfriend wants to have sex. Some people have no sense of priorities.

Pandora's Norwegian Death Metal channel totally sucks.

My grandma accidentally sexted me.

Her sex life is
apparently more
interesting than mine.

My mom FRIENDED me on Facebook.

Mom +

Mom

My mom **UNfriended** me on Facebook.

Nobody "liked" my status.

Just bought a Llama Farm!

 Unlike

Couldn't torrent latest version of my favorite game. Had to actually buy a copy. With real money!

Saw my therapist
at an AA meeting.

My ex has been showing up at my favorite bar. Now I have to drink at home.

Drop-down menu should have the U.S.A. at the top.

Why should I have to scroll past all these countries **nobody** has ever heard of? United Arab Emirates? Is that even a place?

I have to "press one" for English? REALLY?

My password expired.
I LOVED THAT PASSWORD.

PC load letter.

Slow wiper setting is too slow.

Fast wiper setting is too fast.

No cupholders.

Bummed a smoke.

It was a
MENTHOL.

weldon**owen**

President, CEO Terry Newell
VP, Publisher Roger Shaw
Executive Editor Mariah Bear
Creative Director Kelly Booth
Art Director William Mack
Production Director Chris Hemesath
Production Manager Michelle Duggan

Weldon Owen would also like to thank Ian Cannon
for editorial help. Jenna Rosenthal, Hayden Foell, and
Sarah Edelstein provided design assistance.

BONNIER

Library of Congress Control Number
on file with the publisher
ISBN 978-1-61628-410-7
10 9 8 7 6 5 4 3 2 1
2012 2013 2014
Printed in China by 1010 Printing

All illustrations courtesy of Gemma Correl
gemmacorrell.com